LIFE'S MESSAGES AND MUSINGS

Chris Hills

Published 2024: Golden Child Promotions Publishing Ltd

Portland House, Belmont Business Park, Durham,

DH1 1TW

Onlygold@goldenchildpromotionspublishing.com

Copyright © 2024 by Chris Hills

All rights reserved. No part of this publication may be reproduced, stored in a retrieval system or transmitted in any form or by any means, electronic, mechanical, photocopying, recording, and/or otherwise without prior written permission of the publishers.

This book may not be lent, resold, hired out or otherwise disposed of by way of trade in any form, binding or cover other than that in which it is published, without the prior consent of the publishers.

CONTENTS

Introduction — 6

Part 1: Love Experience — 8

- Distant Horizons — 12
- Things Get Better — 14
- Strain — 16
- Memories — 18
- Questions — 22
- Others — 24
- I Know Love — 28
- Happy Now? — 30
- Daytime Lover — 34
- Just A Dream — 38
- Come Home — 42
- You Said We Were Soulmates — 46
- Destiny and Angels — 50
- Dreaming of Love — 54
- Things Went Wrong — 56
- Who's The One? — 60
- Love Unfolds — 64
- Feelings — 66
- There You Were — 68

Tomorrow	70
If Love Is	72
Ever Growing Love	74
Dream Fulfilled	76
Part 2: Conscious Musings	**80**
Can't You See?	84
Spirit Rising	86
Into The Light	88
Seven Tasks	90
Me, Not Them	92
Mankind Gone Mad	94
I Cry	98
Man Un-Kind	100
Warriors	102
Afterword	105

INTRODUCTION

This is a collection of writings gathered over many, many years.

I am not a prolific writer and cannot sit down and just write. There needs to be an inspiration. It might well be another fifty years before another collection is created.

This book, Life's Messages and Musings, is divided into two sections: my love experience and conscious learning, with general musings randomly placed within the sections.

The musings are just random thoughts or something that started that might never grow into something else – a statement of thought.

I am not sure if you, the reader, have experienced similar things or even my life's pattern. I look upon my own life from this place in time. It seems to have followed a roughly similar pattern to the astrological ages: starting in the golden age of being a child, flowing into a silver age followed by a period of bronze age and the dark age itself before beginning its climb back with learning all the way.

My life's journey has brought me to a place where I am content. My knowledge continues to grow and is fuelled by others. You might suggest that I have entered my golden age again.

Enjoy,

Chris Hills

"I'm glad we found each other, and it is what it is and will be what it is meant to be," he said, and he raised his finger to her lips and, from within, he whispered gently without any force, "I love you." The words floated upwards and gently merged into the melody and harmony of the universe as it journeyed through time and space, collecting all the little whispers that would eventually create the whole.

PART 1

LOVE EXPERIENCE

I often wonder how it would have been if you had stayed. Your image appears in every scene as if you were still here.

I have wrestled with my inner understanding forever. Conditioning makes you think you are weird or out of the ordinary when really you are the truth.

You have relationships within the 'norm' and then end up left behind because you cannot conform to expectations. Your spirit is compressed within those relationships because you constantly fight to keep up with expectations that are just not you.

Some people find the balance at whatever level of their consciousness and live together as a couple in harmony. Nothing wrong with that. Problems arise when the harmony is out of balance. It doesn't mean there is no love – you can love deeply and remain deeply in love no matter the outcome of a relationship, another thing that 'others' cannot understand. Why is there an expectation that love has to end with a relationship? The reason you came together was through love, and the only reason we are here is to love and spread love.

Every single one of us is asexual in perfection – perfect balance and harmony becoming a whole. There is no male and female in spirit form. The provision of sexual organs is for the purpose of creating more of us – our physical bodies that carry us through this journey of learning and enlightenment. It is a vehicle created that the spirit then uses for its journey. In times of pleasure, the physical connection (when in unison with the spirit) completes the whole through a physical bond.

We are all free spirits (when awake and knowing) and connected to the 'Whole,' the 'Source,' the 'God,' the 'Light,' the 'Love.' We are one with nature, one with the earth, one with the universe, and one with one another – there is no division, just a life of lessons before we return home to where we live and have lived eternally.

> From the depths of sadness
> Came a shining light
> When I was at the bottom
> You came into my life
> You showed me there is a way
> And I have more to do
> You showed me there is another
> And that, my sweet, is you.

DISTANT HORIZONS

Distant horizons, dreams unfounded
Dark secrets deep inside
A message of love, your feelings rebounded
An old heart that sometimes cries
Too often.

I should know by now how to keep things more guarded
Because for you, love and unhappiness are never parted
A wish for something known but forsaken
Feelings deep inside

Never given a chance to pass yourself on
Too much love and devotion for only one
An emotional weakling
One who wants to give and take more love
Go on, search, keep on seeking.

Selfish and thoughtless, is what you have not enough?
Searching for someone to share your thoughts
You'll never be satisfied
Some unwilling to accept your faults
Mostly take you for a ride.

Is anyone capable of filling empty spaces?
Is anyone stupid enough?
Someone who cares and is selfless. Is anyone really stupid enough?
Wait, your time will come, maybe another lifetime.
But one day, one time, there will be someone, but is it you?

THINGS GET BETTER

We watched, talked, waited, and took our time
And now, when you look at us, we get on real fine
I've really enjoyed the moments we share together
And now they can only get better and better.

Yes, I'll miss and think of you when you're not here
I'll bring you to my dreams, and then you'll be near
Come to me sometimes and share in my dreams
Remember that life, maybe, is more than it seems

Be honest and open. Try and read all the signs
Treat us with pleasure to ensure only good times
We've started something; I don't want to be misunderstood
If we move carefully, it really can be very good

People's most precious assets are their hearts and soul
Protect and treasure them as the bond continues to grow
Don't be afraid. Bring the feelings to the surface
Above all, make sure that we have a purpose

Never to part, our souls together
You and me… forever and ever.

STRAIN

Tugging and pulling, emotions suffer the strain
The strain of loving so much causes the pain
The pain of loneliness, longing, and need
The need to escape and have my heart freed

Freed from a life of depression and despair
Into a life of loving, hope, and care
To care for someone who holds and shares your soul
Someone so important she's become part of your whole

You want her, you need her, to you, she's all and all
To be as one, to share your lives, will she answer your call?
Will she give you more than hints? Will she tell her mind?
Just give her some consideration and more time.

My life is yours, have faith, know it's all for true
Trust and give me more; all I want is a special clue
There is this wait; we need the time but know it's all worthwhile
There's only you, tell me more.
Go on… make me smile.

MEMORIES

Special memories that form in the mind
Forming thoughts into special dreams
Closeness you thought you would never find
Life's never as simple as it seems

You remember things that seem so small
Never realizing how important they can be
It's nice to have something special to recall
When you're not near or around to see

I don't think you know how important it was
That you were around at that certain time
Present not judging, just listening – because
It sorted out, and you made everything fine

Infatuation is a thing of the past
There's nothing to confuse my mind
The closeness we share is more… it will last
I don't know why I was so blind

Memories are little things to remember.
Here are some of mine to share
I'll hold them close to me forever
Because for you, I really do care.

Your smile
Your eyes
Your laugh
Your happiness
Your warmth
Your care
Your touch
Your smell
Your spirit
Your soul

My best and most special friend
Someone who's grown so close I don't want to be without
You, my darling, are a very special and precious treasure, and
I love you in a very special way.

QUESTIONS

It's hard being in love and feeling as I do
A heart torn between not one, but two
Feelings of longing and wanting to be with you
Leaves me in despair, not knowing what to do

This could last more than a lifetime
This could last more than forever
Please be patient; give me time
The decisions I make can only be mine

You never mention your feelings
What's going on inside?
Is this just on one side?
Or is there more beside?

To leave something secure, something so safe and sure
A life of commitments, a life that's such a bore
But, at the moment, for something that only promises more
Tell me your feelings; what do you want to see?

Do you see a future, a life with you and me?
Can you see us happy… will it be the same?
If it becomes more serious, more than just a game,
Will this be the last love that we both share?

Will we be more careful, treasure, protect and care?
If I give up everything, it has to be for real
It has to be forever; my soul cannot take more pain
The hurt will kill it forever. I think I'll go insane.

OTHERS

The 'other' person's position is always the hardest part
A relationship forms; you wish sometimes it didn't start
The 'others' share things that leave you yearning
Your mind's mixed up; your heart starts burning

You want to phone
You want to call
But there you sit, thinking, longing, that's all
You know there's something (special) keeping you together
A bond between you, precious moments to keep forever

At any moment, you want to kiss and hold
You know you daren't even be that bold
You leave the thoughts of love in your mind
Wishing life had been a little more kind

But, you know, he feels the same way too
He wants to love, hold, caress, and be with you
His thoughts flow almost exactly the same way
He hears and treasures everything you have to say

Needing some time with you, he sits there yearning,
Watching, feeling, thinking – always learning
Looking for a sign to show you love him
A reason for the state that you've both got in

But trust him; what you have will last forever
He loves you deep - treasure the moments together
Go for it; don't worry, you can be sure
Every bit you give makes him love you more

        He needs you badly
        He loves you madly

I KNOW LOVE

Oh, I know love
I know the feelings inside
I know when I'm alive
Yeah, I know love

You're the reason I survive
You're the reason I'm alive
Your love is a special thing
Your love makes my heart sing

Your love is special moments
A look, a smile
A thought from a mile
A laugh, a joke
A feeling of hope
A cuddle, a hold
A story retold
A giggle, a move
A life running smooth

Oh, I know love
I know the feelings inside
I know when I'm alive
Yeah, I know love

Everybody needs someone to live for
Nobody could ever love you more
I'm the one who shares your heart
We're the ones who'll never part

HAPPY NOW?

Here you are
You've played around
Let people's feelings rebound
Are you happy now?

Selfish, insecure, and incomplete
A life full of cunningness and deceit
Broken hearts all around
Promises of love they never found
I hope you're happy now.

But now it's your turn,
Torn between love and love
Making prayers to Heaven above
Like how it feels?
I hope you're happy now.

Like the feelings of loneliness and need?
How's that feel compared with greed?
Still have no single regret?
This is something you won't forget.
I hope you're happy now.

So what are you gonna do?
Sort out your life?
Leave your wife?
Cause more pain?
Wish it were still the same?
I hope you're happy now.

What about the other person? Do her feelings count?
Does she let hopefulness mount?
So what are you gonna do? Hurt her too?
I hope you're happy now.

Or does she mean more?
Is she what's been for sure?
Is she the one to fill your heart?
Are you never gonna part?
I hope you're happy now.

DAYTIME LOVER

I'm your daytime lover
And I know the pain
I'm here with another
But things are not the same

With you, I want to be
Please never, ever, desert me
My life just seems to be a mess
I miss your warmth and tenderness

But what can we do?
You know how I feel for you
I live and breathe for you
Our moments together are too few

Lying here thinking of us forever
But snatching only moments together
The time we spend goes too fast
I really hope our love will last

Don't give in; somehow, we'll survive
One day our time will arrive
Put your trust in destiny and fate
Wherever, whenever, it's never too late

But what can we do?
You know how I feel for you
I breathe and live for you
Our moments together are too few

My love for you runs very deep
It hurts my soul and makes me weep
My love for you is very true
My darling, I want to be with you

Keep me close and never let me go
Daytime love can only run slow
Someday we'll spend the night
Everything then will be all right

I'll have you
And you'll have me
Together, forever, our love will be.

JUST A DREAM

It was just a dream from the other day
Just a dream the other day
Just the other day
The other day

I thought you were going to say you'd stay
But the message that you gave me today
Was that you were going away
You're going away

We fought to keep the love alive
But deep inside, we knew it died
And that was only yesterday

So now you're on your way
Sometimes dreams just pass away
Don't look back on yesterday

So this is what you will do
You'll find a life with someone new
Someone new

There'll be someone new for me
Someone who was meant to be
Someone who makes my spirit free
Someone who wants to be with me
Someone for an eternity

It was just a dream from the other day
Just a dream the other day
Just the other day
The other day

You can go on saying what you want to say
It was just a dream that faded away
Just a dream that faded away
Just a dream
A dream.

COME HOME

Come home to me
And set my spirit free
Come home to me
And let us be
One instead of two in harmony

There was a time
When you were mine
But now you've gone away
I tread the path
But see only the past
And hope you'll come back to stay

Come home to me
And set my spirit free
Come home to me
And let us be
One instead of two in harmony

You look and see
But it's not me
Please come home
Don't want to roam
Just sit and long for the day

Come home to me
And set my spirit free
Come home to me
And let us be
One instead of two in harmony

Come home to me
And set my spirit free
Come home to me
And let us be
Again, one and not two in harmony

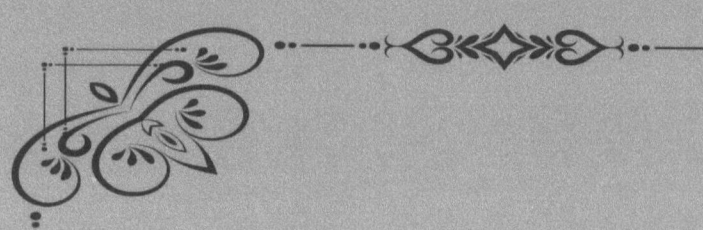

YOU SAID WE WERE SOULMATES

You said we were soulmates
When it was me and you
We said we were soulmates
But how can that be true

We had a wonderful journey
Driven by the heart
Just a temporary journey
Destined to come apart

Soulmates only for a season
And we completed the task
And then there was a reason
We came to the end of our path

You said we were soulmates
When it was me and you
We said we were soulmates
But how can that be true?

Twin flames are for eternity
And we will search for our twin
Spirits together for eternity
Then true love, we will win

Twin flames come and go
As they travel through the stars
Twin flames always know
They'll never be apart

You said we were soulmates
But how can that be true?
We said we were soulmates
But now it's me and you

You said we were soulmates.

DESTINY AND ANGELS

So the evening runs slowly, going to and fro
I've run out of ciggies
Can I be bothered to run to the shops?
No

Awaken in the morning and look at the shop
How strange it's shut
Does this make sense?
I somehow think not

Eventually, it opens, ready for a sale
I make my way over
Return, and now here's a funny tale

As I walk through the gate, she arrives
Why is she here?
It's a complete and utter surprise

She comes and makes herself at home
No ciggy smell, photos she eyes
Destiny played a hand, had it known?

You came into my life
At a moment unforeseen
You came into my life
But was it just a dream?

With timing from above
When I was at a low
You showed me that my inner love

Could still openly and freely flow

It was just sister and brother
The bond just seemed to grow
There was still another
But how was I to know

Someone who shares your heart
Someone by your side
Someone who you still consider a part
Feelings you cannot hide

I'm glad it was a little mistake
Because it made things really clear
And now I can truly relate
And not wait for wrong to appear

I teetered on the edge of hope
That something with us would grow
I put it in the things I wrote
But I guess it won't be so.

DREAMING OF LOVE

Where's love's dream?
Dreaming of love

Fragile, we walk on tiptoe
Delicate, we tread the rim of love
Ghostly, the breath passes by
Dreams pass, off they fly
Another bites the dust

Alone again to wander
Search the shore and look
Treasure's somewhere in your book
Maybe, beneath your foot
Lift your eyes and smile

Love lies waiting
No good wasting
Just live for good
And hope.

THINGS WENT WRONG

And I look to the sky
With a tear in my eye
Things went wrong
You've been gone too long

There was love all along
And then things went wrong
You stayed away
And began to play
It became too much

It broke my heart
To think of us apart
But I had to go
To heal the sorrow
It became too much

And I look to the sky
With a tear in my eye
Things went wrong
You've been gone too long

There was love all along
I know things went wrong
Followed thrills I found
I played around
I was out of control

I know I broke your heart
I thought we'd never part
I took more and more
Moved the thrills to the fore
But I was a fool

And I look to the sky
A tear in my eye
You broke the trust
For excitement and lust

And I look to the sky
With a tear in my eye
Things went wrong
You've been gone too long

You left me lonely and in despair
With a heart I can't repair.

WHO'S THE ONE?

Who's the one?
Here as a part
Who holds my heart

Who's the one?
Here as a part
Who holds my heart

I want a real woman in my life
Someone full of passion
And doesn't care about fashion
Someone who loves me for what I am
And not what they want me to become

I want a real woman in my life
Someone who wants to care
And who is always there
Someone who's by my side
And makes the dreams alive

Who's the one?
Here as a part
Who holds my heart

Who's the one?
Here as a part
Who holds my heart

I want a real woman in my life
Someone who holds me tight
And there to share my light
Someone to share my soul
And make me feel whole

Who's the one?
Here as a part
Who holds my heart

Who's the one?
Here as a part
Who holds my heart

Who's the one?

LOVE UNFOLDS

Thoughts that unfold before my very eyes
A story of love that slowly unwinds
Romantic moments make gentle feelings flow
Gentle feelings that are tossed to and fro

Reeling from what could possibly be
A love that could roam long and free
Free, only if it's nurtured and embraced by you and me
Never forcing it to be something that we cannot see

Something it's never destined to become
'Caus that would leave us hurting and numb
Exciting and different to which we will succumb
Loving, never tasteless, and always plenty of fun

When we are together, fantasies we can share
Secrets to treasure forever that show we are a pair
Always controlled and always fully aware
Every moment filled with love and care

Maybe I'm dreaming but, no, this was foregone
Let's keep it going… carry it on and on and on
Destiny determines that it will be erelong
Love will truly blossom, and it will be so strong

Strong and grow into something that is very replete
Fulfillment and happiness – a life now complete
Can I call you my Nubian Queen?
Because it feels good and expands my esteem.

FEELINGS

A heart that beats faster and faster
A soul that comes alive
A head full of smiles and laughter
A bubbling from inside

Feelings that are comfortable and warm
Wanting to just be with you
Images that in the mind can form
A connection that's still there too

Missing you when you're not here
Constantly in my thoughts
Sensing your presence when you are near
Accepting little faults

Looking forward to any time together
Moments far too few
A longing for it to last forever
Not knowing what to do

It's difficult to understand this thing
But this is what I feel
Let's see what time and fate will bring
Now we know it's real.

THERE YOU WERE

There you were
Shades of darkness and light
Sometimes you scared me
But then something happened that night
Our spirits entwined
And then I knew
It would only be light
For me and you
I think about you a lot
Holding you, just holding you.

TOMORROW

The breeze you felt that passed you by
Rose your eyes up to the sky
And there you saw a shining light
That told you things would be all right
You'll leave the old and start anew
And then be one of the lucky few
Who finds the path to what is real
And open doors to feelings you feel
That never really surfaced

Excitement teeters in tomorrow's day
Who knows what either one will say?
Some new learning fresh to the ear
Time draws close and is very near
Oh no, there's sleep in between too
But I look towards some time with you
And tomorrow is the day.

IF LOVE IS

I want to take you in my arms
And love you for eternity
To be in that special place
Meant for just you and me

If love is in your mind
Believe it
If love is in your heart
Show it
If love is on your lips
Say it
If love is in your soul
Share it.

EVER GROWING LOVE

Ever-growing love…
From the initial stages of attraction to the growing bond…
From the shared emotions, beliefs, and interests…
To the closeness when two thoughts become one…
The point where neither surprises the other, and things are done in union without forethought or knowledge…
No matter the distance or lack of physical presence, the spirits entwine to a point where they travel together outside of the physical realm…

There is always a longing for the physical, but also the knowledge that this little moment in time is nothing compared to what has gone, been, and always will be…
The foundations are deep and strong and can withstand anything that is built upon them…
Friendship, Trust, Unity, and ever-growing love…

DREAM FULFILLED

Gentle the wind of love that blows
Amazing the feelings that are now exposed

The surges of love come open and free
We are in the place of our destiny
In the place I always dreamt would be
Where we would become you and me

Longing for moments when it will be more
There is no one like you, that's for sure
There is no one else - you are the one
My dream fulfilled - I love you hun

PART 2

CONSCIOUS MUSINGS

Life is a collection of circles that replicate the universe and spirit. There is no negativity; it is an invention of man. Zero is absolute, infinite, and of course, whole – It is the one. Even the spelling of one begins with it. The image itself represents the whole, the one.

We have circles of life and circles of spirit – sometimes, they exist together in a physical form.

The circles of spirit are eternal, and we often gather in the subconscious when there is no outside influence to control the physical form: Our spiritual inner and outer circles discuss and plan our physical interactions.

The circles of life are predetermined. As a family, we all planned how it would be: How we would meet, how we would help one another, and how we would exist in a physical form. Think about the instances of déjà vu and how your inner instincts work.

How can you explain how you come together with someone in some way and feel that you have always known him or her? How do you explain a bond that forms in the most unusual, sometimes impossible conditions? How do you explain the same thought or feeling processes that take place? How do you explain that it is often a need of your own and something from which you learn or heal that brings people together?

Life's a journey of lessons towards a determined goal of enlightenment. We meet with soul mates from our soul family so they can help us for a reason or season. We rarely meet our twin flame here, and if we do, it might be a glancing pass or, ultimately, a joining, and then you'll know your spiritual form is complete. You'll know them because they are the mirror of you - you become one.

CAN'T YOU SEE?

You stupid, stupid people (not all of you).
Can't you see?
We weren't meant to be put in boxes and controlled.
We all came from the one.
We all have the same elements as the universe and the world itself.
We were given Eden to enjoy, not destroy.
Why do you let it continue?
Are you blind?
Do you not value the life of another?
Or have you just lost those feelings?
Replaced with objects to care for
Instead of your own type.

SPIRIT RISING

Let the light raise you high
Like the sun warms the sky

Let your light shine bold and bright
Your third eye now has all the sight
All you ever need to know
Is buried like the plants in snow
Switch off the left and wake the right
Allow the thoughts to flow through the night

The sun will warm
And salts will flow
The seeds will grow
And then you'll know
The life you were meant to live

We need to know
We need to grow
We need to care
We need to share
We need to love
We need to reach above

Take care when the moon is in your sign
And release the oils of life so they will climb
All you need is there to heal
Believe, for it is real

The only temple is you alone
The stairway to take you home.

INTO THE LIGHT

And there you are
Lying in the west
You never even knew
What you'd find in the east

You forgot the importance of three
And the person you could really be
You forgot about the cross
Because of all the dross

It's never too late to rise
And look toward the skies
To achieve what you need
Just nurture the seed

You decide where to go
Because now you're in the know
A journey of the best
Into the east and from the west

And slowly, you move
From the darkness and cold
And into the light
With your sun shining bright.

SEVEN TASKS

From the depth of night
You languished in fright
Not knowing which way to go

Searching the door to the stair
You found the wall bare
Still not knowing which way to go

Something took your arm
Without any harm
And showed you which way to go

You saw the light
Shining above bright
And you knew where you had to go

There were seven tasks
That you had to pass
And then you'd begin to know

No more depth of night
Only freedom and light
And then your spirit would flow.

ME, NOT THEM

I don't like this way
I have to spend my day
I want to be a wanderer

I want to reach for the sky
I want to open up my eye
I want to see things clear
I want my ears to hear
I want to bathe in the light
I want to be in the right
I want my spirit free
I just want to be me

I don't like this world
And what I've been told
I want to be a free man

I don't want to be contained
I want the real me to remain
I don't want to live below
I want to be in the know
I don't want to fight
I just want things right
I have so much to give
I just want to live

Mankind Gone Mad

Mourning the parted
Our spirits united
We'll be together again

Love ending
Greed spreading
Mankind gone mad

Peace failing
Wars engaging
Mankind gone mad

Ice melting
No one helping
Mankind gone mad

Birds falling
Insects swarming
Mankind gone mad

Fish dying
Nature crying
Mankind gone mad

Fault lines boiling
Hurricane warnings
Nature trying to mend

Heavens sending
Prophesy ending
Universe taking control

Warnings many
Truth the enemy
Mankind sadly blind

Spirits rising
A few surviving
Mankind left behind

Spirit alive
I'll soon arrive
Mourning the parted

Our spirits united
We'll be together again.

Image by: pxel_photographer-17831348/Pixabay

I CRY

I cry for humanity
I cry for my sanity
Just look at the profanity
And all of the vanity
As they apply their bestiality
And create laws for their abnormality
They revel in their majesty
A world of inhumanity
A complete travesty
A world of depravity
A world with no morality
A world filled with fatality
Watched with complete apathy
It's a real calamity
But it's not finality
Let's fight this insanity
Bring back normality
Destroy the unreality
And live together happily
Stop the territoriality
Show some hospitality
Embrace congeniality
Think about universality
Learn about spirituality
And then praise humanity
For achieving morality
As we live together as one.

MAN UN-KIND

A group of heartless idiots
That think it's fun to take a life
Take a life of a fellow human
Or take a life of another type
They think their crimes go unpunished
But, no, they will not get away free
All is noted in judgment, you see
There is no hope for man un-kind
None of them to save
End this mess and start again
Or just write off all of this kind
There is no love to savor
Bring them to an end.

WARRIORS

The stallion rose with its feet to the sky
We all thought he was going to fly
A warrior upon his back began to ride
With an army of awakened by his side
But only some, the truth could see
The others just fell upon one knee
Thought they had seen something divine
But he was not something to enshrine
He was something to be ever revered
As then, the true image slowly appeared
And the masses joined the march to freedom...

Artist: Petar Meseldzija
(https://www.muddycolors.com/2012/02/authenticity-and-fairytales/).

All writings © 1990 - 2014 Christopher Hills
- All Rights Reserved

AFTERWORD

"Don't talk to me from behind a mask of sincerity because I can see and feel what is truly inside. Talk to me straight and I promise to learn if there is a need. And, if there is no need, I will bear no malice because my own beliefs are strong and have taught me to be tolerant in the company of fools."

- Chris Hills

www.ingramcontent.com/pod-product-compliance
Lightning Source LLC
Chambersburg PA
CBHW041724070526
44585CB00006B/137